I was impressed with Dr. Cassandra McDonald from the moment I was introduced to her and her work. While Dr. McDonald's depth and breadth of education and experience is a dynamic tour de force, she is also the most sensitive, nurturing author a reader could hope for. She brings her deep personal understanding and knowledge to the reader with clarity, offering immediate and practical application of her insights.

Dr. McDonald is clearly on key when she teaches skills that parents can learn and duplicate with their children, and she hits all the right notes. On the list of individuals whose influence I would have gladly brought to the lives of my own children, I would be proud to place the name of Dr. McDonald. Read what she has to say. Listen carefully. You will hear the finest of lessons that come both from the halls of research, and the from the depths of a very great heart.

Shad Helmstetter, Ph.D.
Million-Selling Author of
What To Say When You Talk to Your Self

This is a must-read for any parent or for anyone who has a role in shaping the development of children. Dr. McDonald combines common sense principles and well-researched evidence that remind us that what we say and model for children matter. This book encourages us to use our words and actions to empower children to identify their own gifts and grow with the confidence that they can make meaningful useful contributions to our society. This is a message that is much needed to ensure the future of our society.

Felecia Jones Ross, Ph.D.
Associate Professor, The Ohio State University

So I am asked, "Who is your children's piano teacher". I always pause. How do I answer this simple question when I say to myself, "she's not just a piano teacher. I cannot just simply say "Dr. Cassandra McDonald" because that's not enough. Yes, she is my children's piano teacher. But she doesn't only teach piano, she plays many instruments, she's a recording artist, an operatic professional singer and a performer.

But still, that is not enough. Dr. Cassandra has obtained a PhD in Behavior Science and Family Studies. She is a Certified Life Coach- Self-Talk Trainer, a Motivational Speaker, an Interventional Strategists and a Pentecostal Minister. All these accomplishments have made her qualified as an expert in dealing with children and the family unit.

Witnessing her discipline, knowledge and techniques first hand with my own children while taking piano lessons over the years, I can attest to her brilliancy and successful teaching methods. She understands children, how they learn, and how to teach them in a way they will understand and grasp new material quickly. She knows how to motivate and keeps my children interested in piano, increasing their self-esteem and confidence. She also suggests appropriate discipline, methods and strategies to change bad or unwanted behaviors. She applies her expertise during a one hour lesson in a way we don't expect from <u>just</u> a piano teacher. She is always creative in her approaches, a brilliant woman in which we always come out learning something other than just a piano lesson.

We are your typical normal family. I know that Dr. Cassandra McDonald has been asked to counsel trouble children while in jail, taken them under her care and has successfully turned their life around. She was asked to be on a reality show, aired in Australia and New Zealand, "World's Strictest Parent", that was filmed here in her hometown of Zanesville, OH featuring two independent children whose parents and society have given up on them. She had them live in her home, under her rules & discipline with remarkable success. Not only does she counsel our community's troubled children but also the less fortunate children, locally and abroad. She currently opened a school in Guatemala for children who are orphaned or homeless. She has provided those services and learning opportunities, they would not otherwise have. Currently, her talents have taken her to open her own Academy, which is a Learning Center for Autistic children. I have heard of her successes in motivating and getting "atypical" children to respond to her while no one else could not.

This is a must read for those who do not have the opportunity to hear her speak. There is too much to learn with easy approaches and solutions to problems that we commonly have with our children.

Elena Nicolozakes MSNA, CRNA

Dr. Cassandra McDonald gives her insight into raising successful, happy children – no matter what current challenge parents might be facing. Her upbeat approach and numerous life examples encourage parents in creating a supportive family atmosphere where every child shines. McDonald's positivity channels into practical and doable tips for developing creativity, gentleness, trust, and independence with children. She shows how self-talk connects to a child's actions; and how parents can use this to foster confidence in children. The author's extensive expertise on child development and education provides a foundation for showing parents how obstacles are only a gateway to possibilities with creative vision. This book is a must-read for all parents looking to realize their child's greatest potential.

Alice Walters LMSW, MATS

Ten Ways to Help Your Child Overcome Obstacles

Ten Ways to Help Your Child Overcome Obstacles

Dr. Cassandra McDonald

© 2017 Dr. Cassandra McDonald
All rights reserved.

ISBN-13: 9780692889473
ISBN-10: 0692889477

Dedication

This book is dedicated to my parents who poured value into me. Teaching me how to think about what I thought about. My parents instructed me to have a positive attitude. They modeled a great work ethics for me. My parents were raised during the depression and were very hard working. My mother took care herself by herself at the age of 14. She was determined then she would have the best because she would work for it. She started businesses and gave back taking care of many young girls. She helped supported them in seeking skills for their careers. My mother is an extraordinary visionary. It was through her I learned to serve humanity. Through my parents, I learned strategies for parenting my five children. The most essential factor was modeling what you say. Being that example of positivism. No matter what obstacles come and they will come, I saw how to overcome obstacles through faith and hope. That became the foundational imprint for who I was to become. I am very thankful to everyone who had input into my life and grateful for the support in all of my dreams and visions. It has simply been an amazing experience learning who I am through raising my children and helping raise other children. We grow through whom we integrate and are impactful with, giving one to another. As parents, we are the assigned helper in our children's lives. However, as we help them overcome their obstacles we overcome ours.

Contents

Chapter 1	You Can Teach A Mind ... But You Have To You Train A Body	1
Chapter 2	"It's All Good!" Catch your child doing something good!	9
Chapter 3	Develop A Family Footprint: "Put A Stamp On It!" (Cass)	15
Chapter 4	Bring Out the Sunshine	21
Chapter 5	Expectancy: Be what you are – An incredible you! "Stay hopeful for growth" (Dr. Cass).	29 29
Chapter 6	Purpose With Promise	35
Chapter 7	How to Think About ... What You Think About	41
Chapter 8	It's Not Always Right To Be Right	47
Chapter 9	It's A Mind Thing	53
Chapter 10	Can't Go – Can't Grow....Can't Grow – Can't Go	59
	References	65
	Autism: A Parent, A Teacher, A Professor's Perspective	67
	Intervention Specialist: The Teacher – Natasha Abbas	71
	Stress and Health in Parents of Individuals with Autism Spectrum Disorders Jen D. Wong, Ph.D.	79
	References	83

CHAPTER 1

You Can Teach A Mind ... But You Have To You Train A Body

> "You can teach your mind but you have to train the body." (Dr. Cass)

At a very young age, children emulate and model what they see. They are very aware of facial expressions and body language. They respond and react physically and emotionally. It takes repetition and consistency, to connect the mind with the body. Just like the athlete, musician, or dancer, anyone who uses their body, the training is daily over and over again. Mentally they know what to do but the muscle memory of the body is very short, therefore the body has to be trained.

So it is with the young mind. Mental muscles are vital in training a young mind.

It takes repetition and consistency, which are essential for outcome. Teaching means modeling and showing them. <u>From potty training to teaching posture</u>, repetition mixed with patience is vital for success.

*How do your children learn? Every person takes in knowledge differently. There are three ways in which information is transferred: auditory- listening, visually – seeing, kinesthetically –touching. Every child, regardless of their abilities or disabilities, input knowledge in different ways. To find out how to get their attention, one must engage thought process, making it fun to learn. There are different strategies and theories that help in this area. Gardner's (1983) theory of multiple intelligence is one of those theories.

1. Verbal-linguistic intelligence (well-developed verbal skills and sensitivity to the sounds, meanings and rhythms of words)
2. Logical-mathematical intelligence (ability to think conceptually and abstractly, and capacity to discern logical and numerical patterns)
3. Spatial-visual intelligence (capacity to think in images and pictures, to visualize accurately and abstractly)
4. Bodily-kinesthetic intelligence (ability to control one's body movements and to handle objects skillfully)
5. Musical intelligences (ability to produce and appreciate rhythm, pitch and timber)
6. Interpersonal intelligence (capacity to detect and respond appropriately to the moods, motivations and desires of others)
7. Intrapersonal (capacity to be self-aware and in tune with inner feelings, values, beliefs and thinking processes)
8. Naturalist intelligence (ability to recognize and categorize plants, animals and other objects in nature)
(Source: Thirteen ed. online (2004). Tapping into multiple intelligences. http://www.thirteen.org/edonline/concept2class/mi/index.html)

Let us look at it from a simplistic perspective. People can learn eight different ways. Gardner's theory of multiple intelligence purposes that no two people learn the same way. He proposes that there is no dominant

Ten Ways to Help Your Child Overcome Obstacles

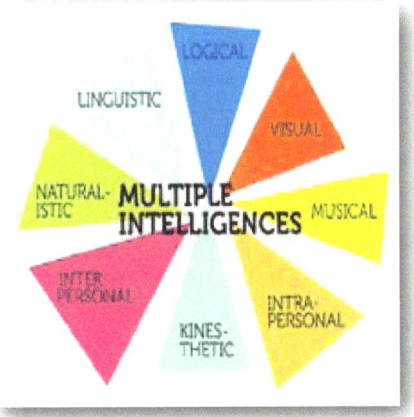 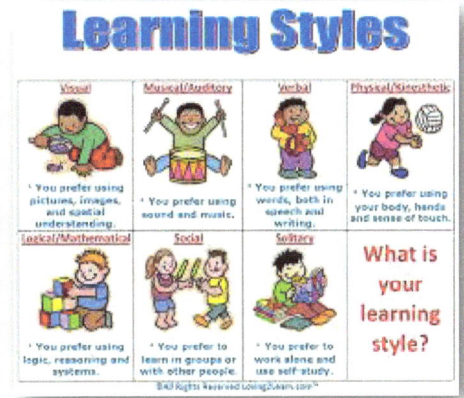

intelligence but multiply ways to magnify one's intelligence. Every child has levels of great intelligence in specific areas. Once you find out what that area is, it can motivate them in other areas as well. If a child is fascinated by rocks, you can use a rock to teach spelling, arithmetic, science, social sciences, reading, et cetera. Actually, you do not even have to come up with the ideas, the child can. Children have such a creative mind, if they are allowed to use that creative mind. They can tell you how the rock relates in those areas.

*** MOST IMPORTANT IS NOT HOW OFTEN YOU GET IT RIGHT. BUT THE TRUST RELATIONSHIP THAT IS DEVELOPED IN THE PROCESS!****

Creative Freedom: How does the child think about what they think about? Do they even think before they do it? What are the results if they do it? Will they respond and react to the way you respond? Parents need to respond positively to their creativity and not react. Give your controlled thinking away. Process before you speak. Receive your child as a blank canvas. Provide stability and a safe creative environment for your child to grow in.

"Think B"

The expressions of adult emotions can appear to be very heavy and very loud to a young child. We must be cautious to be gentle in our actions. Just today, a parent of a five year old autistic boy sent me a picture of where he had used markers on his entire face. Fortunately, they were erasable markers. His face looked like he had a complete tattoo job on every area of his face. Now, in his eyes, he was being very artistic and very creative. So, his mother's reaction was going to be very crucial. Her reaction could destroy his creative artistry or she could make a correction without destroying his heart. His mother was very wise. She took her time. She let a moment go by before responding. She went and got a mirror. The two of them looked into the mirror and had a very good laugh. That moment of silence was "wisdom working". The young man waited to see what his mother would do and how she would react. Sometimes you have to dig really deep into your memory and find the kid you need to remember in you. Just remember your child is exploring.

This is an opportunity to help your child use other avenues of creativity. (Because some of the choices have results, like scrubbing his face and ears and hands vigorously to undo his creativity.)—This sentence is a fragment This is a result that may not be so pleasant and feel so good. So, take the opportunity to share other uses for the markers. Her choice of responding had good outcomes. These are called, "Teaching Moments." So, what you are teaching is logic and rationale. Think beyond the moment of excitement.

Ten Ways to Help Your Child Overcome Obstacles

This is what I call, "Think B!" I learned the little phrase – "Think B," from a cartoon I watched when my children were younger. I raised my children from a very young age through college on the phrase, "Think B." This phrase simply means think beyond the moment. What are the consequences? What are the results? What are the outcomes?

This little cartoon illustration was a little boy who saw his sister with a balloon and he thought to himself, "I will sneak up on her and I'll pop that balloon and it will make her scream won't that be a lot of fun." Then, he began to think, "Hmmm if I pop the balloon and she screams, it will scare the cats. When the cats run through the door, where my mother is making dinner, it could frighten her and cause her to throw the bowl of food into the air. It breaks. The results are I could be in a lot of trouble for a little bit of fun. Maybe it is not worth it at all. Maybe I want to choose another way to have some fun where the results do not get me into so much trouble. Perhaps, I should rethink this and Think B!" I would always say to my children, when they were about to do something, "Think B! Have you thought all the way through your actions? Have you laid out the details and processed the outcomes." I expected them to think!

So, as parents we have to give our children the opportunity to think. Provide opportunities to create rationales. Generate opportunities for them to layout the problem and the consequences and results that one might choose. Give them a chance to be the responsible party for what they do. They need to be prepared to respond to peer pressure. For every action there is a reaction. Each child needs to be equipped with the tools to decide whether this will be a positive or negative outcome. If you stop and think before you do something, then you can control what the outcome is going to be. But as parents we have to sit down, talk to children, and have scenarios where they can think.

Oh Yes!…………..We also need to model this. Is this what they observe us doing???!?

There were times when my children would come and tell me what they wanted to do and ask me what I thought. I would say. "No, I will not answer you. I want you to think about it. Present two justifications A or B. Choose which one has the best and longest results, then come back and we will have a discussion. I want you to think this through."

Most of time, it would result in justifiable creative solutions.

Ten Ways to Help Your Child Overcome Obstacles

The advantages of taking time to train your child how to think are the results. You are preparing them for adulthood. You are not doing all of the thinking for them. My children tell me now they hear my voice in their heads before they make decisions. It reminds them to think through and process the situation. Two other wonderful things: children will know they have the ability and confidence to think through situations and it also builds a relationship of trust which means I can trust them to think through things. This means I trust and respect their opinion about things. When I was coming up, we were told a child was to be seen and not to be heard. We did not have a voice or an opinion. What we thought or said did not matter. We were just to be told what to do because adults knew what was correct and we, as children, did not. I was determined not to use this strategy while raising my children. I wanted them to become responsible children, responsible teenagers, and responsible adults. That meant I had to give them responsibility for them to learn what being responsible meant.

This type of relationship not only builds trust, it builds value in your child's capacity to think. Therefore, when new situations present new issue they have had experience in critical thinking. They are capable of laying out the facts, summating, and creating solutions. It is so important to give your child voice. The reasoning may not be mature but as parents, we can guide and nurture their reasoning. Having those discussions from parent to child, we are also showing what respect is from one human being to another. You must be careful not to talk down to your children as if they really do not have enough sense to make sense. Even a preschooler can come up with things that make good sense. Take time as parents to train. It can be arduous but it breeds success.

Chapter One Notes

1. What is your time commitment for teaching your child?

2. What is your learning style? Your child's may be different.

3. What action will you take to help your child think out loud?

*Please send any questions or topics for discussions to: tenwaystohelp@gmail.com

CHAPTER 2

"It's All Good" Catch your child doing something good!

Use the term... That's good... That's not so good. Replace the word good with bad, terrible, ignorant, dumb, stupid, ridiculous, or phases like, "Have you lost your mind?"

Most of us say to our children, the things that were said to us as children. What were you thinking? Where is your mind? Use your brain. Our parents are repeating what was said to them. This is a cycle that can be very damaging. If you are calling your child descriptive names, framed by their behavior that is how they label themselves. They will identify themselves in their self-talk by saying, "I'm stupid, I'm dumb, I really can't think, I am not very smart." The cycle continues. The reason why people are given names is so they can identify themselves as an individual that has value and purpose.

Parents play a very intricate part of framing their child's self-image, which affects their self-confidence. If the child does not realize that he or she has some value because he or she is not spoken to positively, it can interfere with his or her self-confidence. Catch your child doing something right and praise him or her for it. Surprise them with compliments and positive comments. Be consistent in the way that you talk positive to them. "It's all good," means to say things in a manner that keeps them good as a person but at the same time correct, what they did that was not so good. Use the word "good." Say "That is very good" or "That is not so good." So they continue to be a good person but at the same time recognize that they may not have done things that were good. It also shows them that the not so good things can be corrected.

Improving your self-talk will help you improve your responses while talking to your child. Most typically our self-talk consists of negative that have been said to us and what we say to ourselves. We might say something like, "You never did have a good memory," or "Can't you remember anything?" Being kind starts with being kind to you, then you learn to be kind to others around you. In order to find your child doing something right you have to train yourself to complement yourself then complementing will come easier. For one hour, pay attention and see how many negative and how many positive things you say about you. That will give you a chance to self-evaluate how positive of a person you are.

Were you constantly criticized and judged? Do you criticize and judge? We tend to do the exact same thing that was done to us. You may not intend to but take a moment and observe what it is you do. When I challenged myself to be joyful and positive I found out I was not as joyful and positive of a person as I really thought I was. It took some serious editing of my thoughts before they formed the words so that I could be positive with my children.

Ten Ways to Help Your Child Overcome Obstacles

*Learning positive self-talk is de-programming your negative thoughts and replacing them with positive thoughts. The brain can reset itself. You can develop new directions. Just changing one word in a sentence can change it from being negative. For example: "I do not know." Change that to "I will know" or "I'm going to know." This opens avenues to learn more and gather knowledge and answers. This is a deterrent to not beat yourself up for not having that knowledge. You can investigate, research, asks questions, and at the very least Google!

Words are very powerful and they can do critical damage. You really want to take time and think about what you're saying. Sticks and stones do break bones. Bones heal but words can hurt, sometimes forever. I coach adults everyday who are still telling me words that were said to them in grade school from students and, unfortunately, from teachers that still "drive" their lives today. They have not learned how to release the words that were spoken to them. The great news about self-talk is you can learn how to edit those words and change them into positive thoughts. The reason why they continuously hurt is because we continuously, "Rehearse the Hurt." When those words come to you, simply turn them into a positive statement. I am almost six feet tall and was bullied for being the tallest person in the school. I never saw a student my height until I was in high school. When the words that I was bullied with came to me in high school, I would change those words to, I am tall. I stand out in a crowd and get noticed." Now, even as an adult, I know when I walk in the room there is a certain amount of attention I am going to have because I am tall, so I try to represent myself well and present a joyful spirit.

Some children have stronger spirits and other children do not. Each child may respond in different ways and need different support. We should not say, "I was bullied, and I got over it. Become tougher and get over it." As we know, currently, some children are committing suicide over being bullied. This is completely a new level of communication. So, as parents we have to make sure that we're the most vital and consistent communication that they have. They should know they can come and talk to us. If you are the parent that is not very talkative, find someone that the child can talk to that you trust. It is important that the child has someone to vent and share their emotions and experiences with.

Family Strategies.

(Comparing to other family members. Phrases like: "You are just like your father." People told my daughter: "You are just like your auntie." She wondered what that meant. She had a great relationship with her aunt. Adult relationships are comparably different than children relationships. As a child she could only see the good in people.

Ten Ways to Help Your Child Overcome Obstacles

We have to be careful to not let the fears of our past reflect on how we talk to our children. As adults, we cannot let our bitterness affect our relationship with our children. Example: I heard a mother abusing her four-year-old son verbally saying, "You are just like your father. You are lazy. You will never be anything." I stopped her in the middle of her sentence and pulled her to the side. I told her, "This child is four years old. You are the one who became pregnant, he did not. Do not abuse him because you regret that you went and chose a loser father who is not around to help guide him. You have to encourage him especially because he does not have a father in his life. Why should he grow up with your bitterness? It is your fault and not his. He is a very nice young man. You have done a great job with raising him so far. He is very respectful, very kind, and he has talent. Do not kill him with your words! Use kind words every time he does something wonderful encourage him with that. Build up his self-esteem. With or without a father, let him know he will be successful because you will be supporting him all the way.

Chapter Two Notes

1. Have you caught your child doing something good lately?

2. Do you use positive words to describe your child?

3. What action steps are you taking to promote positive thinking?

*Please send any questions or topics for discussions to: tenwaystohelp@gmail.com

CHAPTER 3

Develop A Family Footprint: "Put A Stamp On It!" (Cass)

FIND A COMMONALITY in your family; a family trait. It may be that you all like music. Maybe a particular height runs in your family. It may be that you are all have curly hair. Perhaps your voices are similar. You love laughing. Most everyone is a good cook. Find something that is unique about your family, then put a stamp on it. This trait represents the family. "You present what you represent. You represent what you present (Dr. Cass)!" Your child needs to be aware that someone is always watching his or her behavior. So, represent yourself and the family well. Think before you speak and before you respond. Pay attention to how you dress and how you groom yourself. Feel good about how you look. Appearance is important. Care about your hair, being clean, and being presentable. You can be stylish with whatever your style is. A statistical fact: people see 97% and hear 3%. Being a well-groomed family is something you can put a stamp on.

> Looking at Human Validation Model: the validation process gives attention to embracing and empowering self-esteem in each family member. Different techniques are used to shed positive light on possibilities and compassion used in family communications (Bitter, Long, & Young, 2010).

In order to create positive patterns you can develop maps like roadmaps. You reconstruct the past to create a positive present. For example: I was bullied because I was so tall. I changed the words saying, "Most everyone in my family is tall. It's a family trait. I speak of it as a positive attribute that I'm proud of." This allowed me to reframe the negative comments from my past, letting go of the emotions that were attached to it. Your child needs you to be proud of you, them, and the family. If that is not possible within the family structure, then find a role model that you both can relate to and be proud of.

Create positive family stories. Most stories about families that I have heard are poking or making fun of an individual and everyone finds that as a commonality. That does not build character or a positive outcome for that person or the family as a whole.

> Narrative family study (White, 1986) houses the fundamental assumptions that our understanding of the world is experienced through structured language and stories that we tell. The stories are the dominant dialogues influenced by society that construct reality. Because stories determine how people think, they shape and define individuals and their perspectives of their future (Dean, 1995).

Ten Ways to Help Your Child Overcome Obstacles

Share positive memories that will influence generations to come. When I met my paternal grandmother's side of the family, they told me a story they gave me such strength. One of their grandfathers was in the war and they were not receiving the monies from the post office. The local government was keeping it. He made his way to the President of the United States to report what was happening. Of course, he was told he could not see him, but he thought, "Everyone has to go to the bathroom sometime." So, he waited until the president went to the bathroom and reported what was going on.. It encouraged me to know my DNA. We do not give up!

Family Games

Have family members make a list of things that they like and dislike. Compare the list at the end of the month. Watch the changes in family members taste and structure develops. This is an opportunity to learn new things about each other. It also creates a way of communicating without having to talk to each other, if you are not very talkative. Make this list without putting names on it. Try to figure out whom the list matches to. You could have popcorn, drinks, and food to make it fun. It need not take more than 30 minutes to do this. This can be an opportunity to support each other in a positive self-valuing manner.

Have each member make a list of five strengths, five interest, five fears to overcome, and five goals you would like to accomplish before the end next of year. Once a month you can do this and change the five things on the list. Ask questions like: What are the barriers, if there are any that you see to distract you from accomplishing these goals? What steps do you need to take to accomplish these goals? This will build character within your family and communication. I have talked with adults who have said no one ever asked them what they wanted to be or what they liked in life. The discussion needs to help each member excel as an individual. So, the question remains…What are you willing to give and what are you willing to receive from your family to make life more pleasant?

Changing is a choice. The mind is the most powerful instrument known to man. Free will is really a choice. In the past scientists agreed, that the brain cannot be changed but now they know you can change your brain with your thoughts. People have done physically impossible things just by setting their mind to those goals. Within our family structure, we want to use our minds to our advantage. As human beings, we are wired to love and to be loved. Anything outside of that causes a stress and affects our health. Recent research shows that most of the diseases are caused by stress. When something goes wrong in the body, the body does not function correctly. Our bodies were created to heal itself, provided we do not interfere. Inhibitors are not enough sleep, rest, water, proper food, and avoiding stressful attitudes.

If you want to change a family structure, change your thinking. Reframe and create something worth putting a stamp on as your family footprints. So many times, I hear parents say, "That is the way I was raised that was good enough for me." That will be one opinion.... Yours! Do you not want better for your children? Do you not want them to have the advantage of your experience and wisdom and to do more? The things that you know can help your child to move forward. We must remember that everyone is different and may need many different applications to be successful. Therefore, the way you have always done it may not work for the child that you have. Because of the access to media, children are exposed to lot things we never even, had to think about growing up as a child. There has to be an adjustment, an accountability to help our children grow up as responsible adults. Our goal is for children to be successful. It is possible. One basic need, that has not changed, is to be loved. For sure, there is love in your family. That is something you can put a stamp on!

Chapter Three Notes

1. What is special about you family?

2. Did you make a new family calendar?

3. What actions have you taken to provide freedom in family choices?

*Please send any questions or topics for discussions to: tenwaystohelp@gmail.com

CHAPTER 4

Bring Out the Sunshine

ALLOW YOUR CHILD to have a voice. Encourage your child to talk about their ideas. Support and confirm them. If you do not like their ideas, become an actor and an actor and say they are very interesting. We all seek approval. Compliments are encouraging. Validation creates confidence. Your child needs to know there is a light in them that makes them unique and special. Self-confidence is required for motivation in pursuing career goals that can be affected by cultural-social environments. Socioeconomic status, beliefs, and perceptions about educational goals can also affect educational outcomes.

Identify Behavior

Identify the behavior of the child but do not identify the child as being the behavior problem. Set age appropriate goals and be consistent. Have expectations for the child to have good behavior. I was identified as a fidgety child, (It is now called ADHD). I was always moving and was never still. My mother took that behavior and focused it in my desire to learn to play the piano. It gave me somewhere to drive that energy. I would play and sing for hours. My mother now says I played when I was angry. I played when I was mad. I played when I was glad. I always played. It was my outlet. Music became my communicative tool. I could identify with it. The outcome is that music became the core my purpose.

I hear adults saying, "What is my purpose? Why am I here?" Start this discovery early in your child's life. Make evolving changes overtime. Work toward identifying something special in your child. Despite the importance of purpose, it remains an elusive construct only beginning to be operationally defined and investigated through research efforts.

> Adolescence presents a formative period of identity development (Erikson, 1950). A sense of purpose is central to negotiating adolescence and laying the foundation for continued success in adult endeavors. The developmental stage of adolescence is a unique opportunity to investigate underlying aspects in the complexity of purpose. This guiding light of purpose and direction is vital.

It is much easier to get to a destination when you know where you are going. While raising my children, my goal was to expose them to as many different avenues in life, allowing them to explore their purpose. I used the public library. It is a resource for directions of where to go and how to get there!

Ten Ways to Help Your Child Overcome Obstacles

Building Trust

The trust, respect, and honor you want to receive from your child is the trust, respect, and honor you must give to your child. These are learned behaviors. If your child was constantly being called negative names and was never listened to, this is exactly how they will treat others and you. It is important that you model and show your child how to exhibit those qualities of character. In doing so, your child will recognize what and how they are to treat people. If you say please and thank you to your child, then they will know that please and thank you are supposed to be practiced. Showing respect can simply mean asking a question and waiting for an answer. When the answer comes from the child it may not be the correct answer, but it is giving the child a chance to develop thought patterns. Now, you can work with the child and help them to understand how these thoughts come together as a critical thinker.

Simply Talk About It

Simply say, "Let's talk about this and look at the possibilities." Perhaps, there are other options and avenues to be considered. It is not necessarily for the child to understand thoroughly but for them to know that they can be heard. Most generally, they have not developed enough cognition to understand. That is why we we should teach our children to listen. Take time to explain your reasoning to the child. This will build trust I have seen reasoning deflate anger. Even though they do not understand, they see that you care about what they think. Trust factor is something that you want to build. Show you care about what they think. After a while the child will start to figure thing out... Instead of thinking, " Here we go with another long, long explanation", they will begin to listen with thought processing. They will begin to make decisions to take a shortcuts and just do what they are asked..

Trust factors

It becomes challenging when you give a directive and the child does not respond to it in a positive way. The child has to trust that you have their best interest in mind. Building trust means that your children know that they do not have to deal with your emotions and their emotions too. Building trust means that they feel comfortable and that you are not upset with them as a person. This task has to be finished. After a while, when you give a directive, they will respond because they know that you will not become emotional and they trust that you still will not be upset with them. Reading their body language helps you to understand what they are thinking. Even though they may or may not be able to verbally express it, look for their body language. This can be a measurement for progress being made when they respond without a pause. Mission accomplished. The trust factor is working. You are observing more outcomes that are positive.

Ten Ways to Help Your Child Overcome Obstacles

Believe In Your Child

Parents model belief towards the children. It is so important to have a child know that you believe in him/her. They hear you when you speak to others about them. So, take time to brag on your child. Take away their fear that you are always mad at them.

They need to know that they can trust you with their private information. They need to believe that you will not criticize and hold it against them for evidence later. Children need guidance and look for guidance. You are their foundation and rock. They need safety, knowing they can depend on you.

That is why children love superheroes. It is a fantasy of power and dependability. Superheroes save the world. You represent that superhero to them. Parents sometimes confuse the position of being a friends or parents to their child. It is not the same thing. You are their parent first and they may regard you as a friend. But, they need know that you are working on being the best responsible parent that will defend, take care of, and be there for them in every situation. Friends are not always available to do that.

I remember being in college and my roommate said braggingly. "My parents didn't care if I did this… didn't care if I did that… actually I don't think they cared about anything or even about me. They just wanted me out of their hair!" Take time with your child. Everything you purchase will become old and out of style. Time is the most important element you can give. Creating memories is essential. It becomes a personal experience. The time that you spend with your child shows them that they are valuable because you believe in who they are. You see the light in them!

Chapter Four Notes

1. How can you help your child have a voice?

2. Have you thought any differently about your child's behavior?

3. What action steps have you taken to build trust?

*Please send any questions or topics for discussions to: tenwaystohelp@gmail.com

CHAPTER 5

Expectancy: Be what you are – An incredible you! "Stay hopeful for growth" (Dr. Cass).

WITH SUPPORT, YOUR child will develop. They will grow. What you see right now is not your child's future. With these tools, that I am sharing, your child will grow and develop. If your child knows that you expect more they will do more. Expectancy breeds confidence. It says, "I expect more from you than this because you are capable of doing more than this." It raises your child's self-esteem, self-value and changes self-goals. Children, like adults, need to know that someone believes in them; someone believes that they can be an incredible person. Children need to know someone sees their talents and have faith and confidence in them. You become, as a parent, that hero that says with an outreached hand….. "You can do this and I will help you, until you do this."

My mother discovered my talent for music. At five years old, she began my private piano lessons. For one year, I practiced on a piece of cardboard with piano keys painted on them. At five years old I had to prove I was serious for an <u>entire year</u>. She had very high expectancies. I would go across the street to Mrs. Butler twice a week and practice on a real piano to prepare for my piano lessons. After one year, my mother decided that I was serious. I came home one day and she had purchased this beautiful baby grand piano for me. I never knew anyone that had a baby grand piano, not even while I was in college. Her expectancy pushed, prodded, and proved me into becoming a serious musician. Wherever I teach and perform, all over the world, I give them my mother's two rules for me.

Rule #1: If I ever have to ask you to practice I will sell the piano. Rule #2: Always be prepared with five piano selections memorized when my company comes. I used the same rules on all of my children. I have five children with five music degrees and thirteen degrees combined in their vocations, as I mentioned earlier.

Having defined lines of expectancy establishes accountability. As a child, there are many things I did not do because I knew they were unacceptable. There were clear consequences. I knew I would have to be accountable for my actions. As I speak to young students now they want to do their homework mainly because of accountability. Producing good grades and meeting expectancy at home, motivates them. They would rather work hard, achieve good grades, than face those negative consequences.

Say what you mean and mean what you say: One of my parents had a high school student who was performing very poorly in high school. She knew her daughter's capabilities were much more than that. But, her daughter was just not inspired and continually brought home very low grades. Her daughter loved the horse that her parents had purchased for her. Her mother said, "Bring up your grades or I am selling the horse." She still did not bring up her grades. I think she realized how serious her mother was when she watched as her mother sold the horse.

Ten Ways to Help Your Child Overcome Obstacles

The mother said that was the toughest thing she ever had to do to her daughter…..But…… Her daughter's grades zoomed up to the top and stayed at the top. I asked her if she ever purchased another horse for her daughter. She said no! Her daughter is now married with children and said she has finally forgiven her for selling her horse. She understands it now completely. It really affected her life and how she is raising her children presently.

> Bandura's theory of self-efficacy was the second theory underlying the present study. Bandura developed this construct to help explain how people control their self-determined judgments and resulting actions. It can also be seen as a personal agency tool that reflects how people feel about their ability to execute various tasks and roles (Bandura, 1989).

If there is no expectancy then there are no goals. Without goals there is no hope. The hope is to meet the expected level of accountability. As adult, when we accept a job in the workforce, we are given the expectations for that job. We are accountable to meet those expectations. Without doing so, there is no reward for our work. This is the same development structure that we should mandate for our children to have. It builds character and confidence.

I just spoke with a high position banker about his children at home. The daughter never has to be asked to do anything. She has great character. She does her work well at school obtaining straight A's. She does work well at home. It is just part of her personality. The younger son is quite the opposite. He attempts to get away with the least amount of effort. The parents are now realizing they did not have any expectations for the son. When his grades started becoming lower and lower, they understood the reflection of no expectation had carried over into school. Now, at 11 years old, they have changed the complete accountability structure of his life. He now has to be accountable for his grades, for his laundry, and for doing chores around the house. It is true that every child is different. But, there has to be a level of expectancy given to each child. Those levels need to be continuously raised each year. As you become older and more mature more should be expected. As you raise the levels, raise the level of time training your child. Do not expect them to just know because they do not. Encourage them; they are teachable and trainable and this is achievable. Tell them, "I expect you to become an incredible you!"

Chapter Five Notes

1. Have you told your child how wonderful and unique they are?

___

2. Have you been true to you words?

___

3. What actions have you take to help your child reach their goals?

___

*Please send any questions or topics for discussions to: tenwaystohelp@gmail.com

CHAPTER 6

Purpose With Promise

Do it on purpose

EVERY CHILD IS a promise and has a promised future. Someone needs to believe that for them and get that message to them. Sometimes there may be other influencers, such as grandparents, uncles, aunts, and teachers. As a parent, approve, support, and encourage whoever is influencing your child positively.

> Realizing one's intelligence can also be accomplished thorough self-efficacy. Self-discovery enables students to achieve balance. Students who believe they are competent have self-esteem. The theory of self-efficacy (Bandura, 1989) supports that one's belief in his or her ability is a direct outcome of one's performance. The environment does influence student development, but students can identify their own integral base through self-efficacy. Positive self-advocacy helps individuals set higher goals and be committed to these goals. When negative feedback comes, it can allow for a more optimistic view and response. Individuals are able to self-reflect and develop internal standards about their capabilities. These thoughts produce self-evaluation, which reflect self-efficacy (Garrin, 2013).

As a private teacher of students, I see them on a weekly basis. For that half hour or hour that I have, I make sure I am packing, empowering, and encouraging them to go as far and as fast as they can. It becomes a

helping tool to a parent to see his/her child in another light. To know that someone sees something more in the child they do can be a realization of hope for that parent. As parents, we are raising a child that we have never raised before. I tell parents, "You are the boot camp leader." Home is their training ground. We must change the culture of how we were raised. Perhaps we were never complimented, encouraged, or received attention. That is not because it was not needed. We now have an opportunity to create a new culture in our family.

Boot Camp

So often, when I give compliments about children in the presence of the parent the parent will say, "Who are you talking about?" I will correct them and say please do not put down your child while I am trying to raise them up. Then, later, pulling the parent to the side I explain how the parent is the boot camp leader for the child. Your home is the boot camp training ground. This is where the child learns how to react or

Ten Ways to Help Your Child Overcome Obstacles

respond in public. Of course, they are going to rebel at home. Home is their stomping grounds. But, the proof that you are doing an incredible job as a parent is when your child is out in public. They respond and react properly with integrity and promise.

I learned this lesson very early on when I had my first child who was a girl. I would play for the live radio broadcast at church. There was a person in the church who would hold my child while I played. One day she brought her to me and said, "This child is perfect with me. She never acts up. She is always pleasant. She is fine and she is quiet. I see she never acts that way with you." My response to her was, "Thank you, thank you, thank you! What an incredible compliment. This means that I must be a wonderful parent and I am training my child so effectively. I am the person, if she's going to act up, that I want her to act up with, so that I can train her. The great compliment is that when she goes with you, all of my hard work and training comes to fruition! Therefore, you have a well-trained baby when you get her. Again, thank you!" As a parent, this was encouraging to me. Seeing this processed promise in my child. She was teachable. Hoorah! Hoorah! Hoorah! I then knew that if I put in the time, effort, love, kindness, and patience, this promise would grow with a purpose that would be potentially powerful!

The Increasing Influences

As our children entered high school, we were told we would become the least influence in their life. The technique of talking so your child will listen and listen so your child will talk, is a strategy I always tried to use.

> Family cultures transmit values from one generation to the next. Seeking family approval often means embodiment of the family's social culture (Gore & Wilburn, 2010). Learners' physiological pathways can be influenced by their family's cultures and social skills based on their reactions to what was done collectively rather than developing individualistic tracts within your family structure (Keller, 2011). This starts when they are young.

Throughout this book, we have been focusing on building a relationship of trust and shared beliefs in each other. My first strategy was this: Four of my children were born in November. I decided to have a party for every child each year. That meant we would decorate the house November first because birthdays started in the second and ended on the twenty-seventh. Each child had their own day of being celebrated. It made them feel special and valuable. My second strategy was this: As a parent, it not only gave me a voice with their friends, but also their friend's parents. Twenty years later, I met my children's adult friends who attended all of the parties. They said they were safe and fun. They waited every year for the party where they could just have fun, be who they were, and enjoy themselves. My intent was to still have an influential voice in my children's lives. I wanted to be a purposeful part in developing the promise in my children.

Ten Ways to Help Your Child Overcome Obstacles

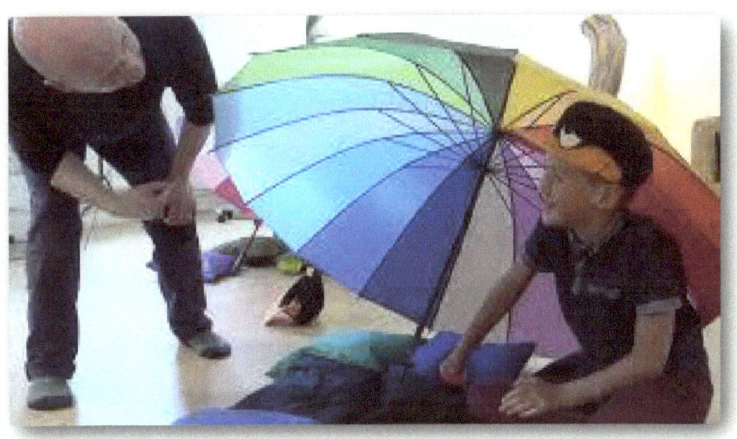

Chapter Six Notes

1. Do you realize what an incredible promise your child is?

2. How are you handling the assignment of being the trainer?

3. What actions are you taking to make sure your child has positive influences?

*Please send any questions or topics for discussions to: tenwaystohelp@gmail.com

CHAPTER 7

How to Think About ... What You Think About.

THINKING IS A controllable process. Positive and negative thoughts come to us all. The thoughts that we choose to nurture, feed, and entertain are the thoughts that grow. The pattern is formulated….Thoughts become words…words become actions…actions become part of our character. Thus there is the future. Change your mind; change your life! This works for anybody, at any age, at any time. Training your thought patterns affect your perception. You can have a positive lens to most any situation if you control your thought patterns. What you chose to think is a choice.

I was told once years ago that no one can make me angry. I had so many scenarios where people have made me angry. They were really the reason why I was angry. I did not understand that anger was a choice. I could choose whether or not to accept the situation. My choices were to work towards resolving it and moving on, or sit in the situation and continue to be angry. Eventually, I began to understand it was a choice. I could choose how I wanted to respond rather than react to the situation. Now, my choices are based on what is healthiest for me. I have learned that to be angry causes me stress. Stress for me affects my health. Do I get upset? Absolutely! But, I give myself some time to de-escalate, refocus, and regroup my emotions. It is a constant training for me to control negative reactions and responses. As your children watch you, they will model their reactions through your responses to them.

We will often say to our children, "I want you to think about what you just did. Take some time and think about it." This is a typical statement. But how do children critically analyze what they did. Generally, if the consequences are strong enough, the only analytical thinking that children do is to conclude that they do not want to do what they did because they do not like the consequence. They were not able, with their cognitive level, to figure out why they should not do what they did. They just know that they did not like the results after doing it. If you want your children to think about what they did, then you have to help them process that. Take time to talk to your children.

Nonverbal students, like any child, like to have their way. Their needs may require more explanations because they cannot verbalize their thoughts. For their thinking process, they may need more explanations of consequences. The results of their actions need to be explained in more detail. Taking the time to explain 'why' helps the child to make more mature choices. What I found out was that it builds trust and value in the relationship. More and more, less explanation was needed. I would observe my nonverbal student stopping and thinking before he would do things. I could tell that he was processing why that action should or should not be done.

Developing the use of the term good, and not good seemed to be effective. It separates the character of a person from the activity performed. What you did, the activity, was not good. It did not affect your good character or person that you are. You simply need to change that behavior. The behavior does not define your character. I shared this concept with parents. Instead

Ten Ways to Help Your Child Overcome Obstacles

of calling your child bad, simply say what he did was bad. He can change his actions from bad to good and still be a good person. Changing from a bad person to a good person could take a lot of refinement. Teaching them how to think about their thoughts improves their behavior. Children learn and process their thinking differently. Some children need a picture painted. They need details to help them visualize their thinking process. So many times as parents we say, "Are you listening to me? Did you hear anything I said?" The child may need more time to process his/her thoughts. Take time and ask if they understood what you said. Do they have any questions?

Critical layering is a process. I was talking with a parent of a child that has now been diagnosed dyslexia. Before the diagnosis, the parent worked with the child fervently. Her grades in school came with such a struggle. The parent and the child both suspected that she was dyslexic, but the parents did not want her labeled. The child also feared finding out because she really did not want to know either. I told the parent that she was protecting herself and not her child. There was a situation that happened at the home. Choices after this incident pushed for the child to be diagnosed. There were heated conversations between the family and the doctor. The doctor, before testing, said she does not have dyslexia. The mother humbly asked the doctor, "Are you always correct?" The doctor said, "I most certainly am." But, after vigorous testing, the results showed that she was dyslexic and several other things. The child responded, "I am so glad to know because at least I know now I am not crazy!"

What a person thinks about themselves is impacts the outcome of how they perform. Having low self-esteem can discourage a person. Trust yourself and your child enough to help them. You have to fight for your child. Children cannot for themselves. It is a difficult task if you need help to ask for help. This is one of the reasons why I am writing this book to let you know that there is help out there.

Self-talk has been explored by Dr. Shad Helmstetter (1982). What you say to yourself really matters. Say positive things about yourself: "I am a winner! I believe in myself. I respect myself. I like who I am." Dr. Shad validates you can create a positive self-image and change your life forever. What you think about impacts the outcome of whom and what you are. You can learn to think more effectively when you learn to think more positively.

At home is where the supportive environment begins to give children confidence in who they are. If they know what they are thinking about and how they think about what they think about it carries over in the school environment. A confident student has a better attitude in focus and career goals.

Maslow revisited (2003) promotes that having the freedom to think and process your thinking is invaluable. According to Keene (2008), higher education not only prepares us to face work challenges but intellectually prepares us for life. The hope is to keep kids in school. Helping students define their learning style, develop a consistency in their test results in retrieving information is one of the goals. Different ways of defining smart help students to define their personal intelligence.

Chapter Seven Notes

1. How often are you editing you thoughts?

___

2. Are you using effective criticism?

___

3. What actions step are you taking to make sure you needs are being meet?

___

*Please send any questions or topics for discussions to: tenwaystohelp@gmail.com

CHAPTER 8

It's Not Always Right To Be Right

CHILDREN HAVE A LANGUAGE OF THEIR OWN.
How DOES A parent validate a child's thinking? How do you help confirm their thinking as part of their identity? How can you help them with their reasoning? How do you support your child when it sounds right to them and it is not logical to you as their parent?

Case scenario with my daughter: This was all about doing the dishes. I observed that my daughter rinsed off all of the dishes before washing them. After placing the rinsed dishes on the counter, she made dishwater. We had double sinks. The left sink was full of soapy clean water and the right sink was the clean rinsing water. She put the rinsed dishes in soapy water; she would scrub them, and then proceeded to dip them in the clean rinse water. I could not believe that she took all of that time to rinse off the dishes to make sure they were perfectly clean before washing them. I proceeded to tell her this was a waste of time. I said, "What do you think the soap is for? It is to clean the dishes." She looked at me and said, "This is how I do it. I like to have clean water." I thought well, "It is not always right to be right." That was one of those times. What I wanted was clean dishes. If she had a different way of doing it, I needed to support her in her thinking. This acknowledgment helped grow her self-identity. She knew that she had certain ways that she liked to do certain things. It made perfect sense to her. This is how she processed her thinking. The outcome was a task done well. These patterns were carried out through other areas in her life. She knows how she likes to do things. She has an order about everything and she is very particular about it. The outcomes are simply wonderful. I learned that you have to allow children to be themselves. Give them permission to develop. It will be a process of patience for you as parents. They were not born to be you, nor will they ever be or do things the way you do as their parent. As parents, we should encourage them to be that individual, unique one-of-a-kind person, that they were created to be. They need to know you embrace this. In doing so, you help build a solid foundation with confidence supporting them to be who they are.

As parents we can see the generational identity traits in our children. We will call these vertical traits, referencing being downloaded through DNA. These traits could be color of hair, eyes, and skin. These vertical traits can also be identified through the physical shapes of their eyes, nose, hands, and feet. Some identities are acquired from peer groups. The horizontal identity can be those cultural ethnic practices and social influences. Then there are conditions that exist with an individual that are not directly inherited. These conditions could be intellectual disability, autism, dyslexia, or attention deficit hyperactivity disorder (ADHD). There are some things within children that trigger these characteristics. How do we as parents adjust? We see these beautiful children and their potential. As parents, we have goals and dreams and visions for each of our children. Do our goals, visions, and dreams match with their goals, visions, and dreams? How do we support them when our dreams and their dreams are not parallel? Are we open to understanding where our children are coming from?

It is so easy to compare your children with others, yourself, or to one of your relatives. It is not easy for children to live up to those comparisons.

Ten Ways to Help Your Child Overcome Obstacles

It is even more difficult for them to feel valuable knowing who they are, is not good enough. How does a child live with the expectancy to carry another person's visions and not their own? If you were raised never having the opportunity to carry out your visions and dreams, break that pattern. Have higher goals for your family.

> Vygotsky's zone of proximal development (ZPD) reflects the distance between one's present learning level and one's potential learning ability. ZPD holds that the educational/developmental process of scaffolding, where social support is provided to move the child to the upper area of the ZPD, is where learning takes place. Therefore, cultural and social influences come to the learner first and then they develop (Vygotsky, 1896/1934). In essence, Vygotsky's ZPD holds that children can learn above where they are developmentally. Students having the same learning experience can move cognitively and developmentally in different stages. Cultural exposure can change the perception of information given (Keller, 2011). Therefore, the developmental process can be slower or faster for the learner because of the relevant connection of the information given. The emergence or recognition of children's developmental processes can be influenced by their intellectual and sociocultural competencies. Bruner (1996) stressed the role that culture and environment play in the development of cognition. Intelligence is defined by social skills and social responsibilities. Expectancies are measured within social status. Within the content of acceptability, there is an increased awareness of the relationship of cognition and environmental context (Bruner, 1996). To gain a different social status would be unacceptable. As an example, for individuals who were raised in a farming community, the expectancy would be to carry on the farming tradition. This can limit their personal self-value and dreams.

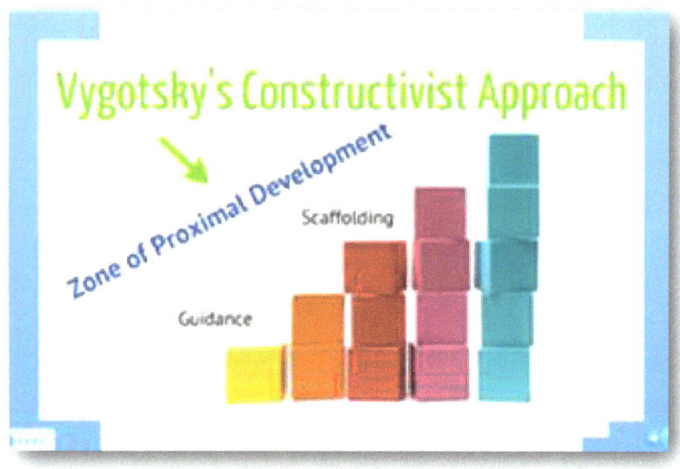

If we are that ambitious and organized parent that has the strong personality, we may not understand why our children may be docile and not aggressive. Their personality does not seem to be overly concerned about anything. They do not multitask. We must carefully refrain from making statements like, "Why can't you be more like… Why can't you do this or that….. I do not understand you." Although these may be true statements that we cannot afford to make them. Words have power. Words hurt. Some things said are unrecoverable. The job of a parent is to train children, support them, and uplift them to become stable individuals as adults. This is a really big job! Do not fear, this does not have to be accomplished in one year. The key factor is to communicate. Do not be afraid to let your children see you as a human being that makes mistakes. They will respect you for not being perfect.

I told my children, "I am learning how to raise you. There are some things that are in my history that I do not want to repeat in raising you. So, I am trying to work through that. If I am wrong, tell me. Find a respectful way to do it. But talk to me." My four boys were straightforward: "Mom we need to talk". My daughter's strategy was she would become very quiet. She would not have much to say to me at all. Then, I knew I had done something. So, I would ask her to tell me what it was that I done. Her points would be very valid. I had not looked at these issues from her perspective. We would then cry and laugh together getting it straightened out. I made a habit to say, "Please, thank you, and I am sorry," if it was needed. I wanted them to know that their opinions and their thoughts were important and valued. I love the fact that my grown children tell me now that they knew that they had a voice. Their voice was heard. That was a goal I worked very hard for. I wanted them know that they were valuable. I know that was a key factor in developing close relationships that still exist presently. We still have great communicative skills and share. We trust each other's judgments and value each other's opinion. That is the cohesiveness I wanted as a family.

As parents, we want to train our children to be responsible adults and think through situations. This includes building their individual character and equipping them to integrate into a societal system that may or may not make allowances for individuality. Yet, we want our children to have the stability and confidence to think through the process knowing their self-value. We want our children to stand in their self-integrity.

Chapter Eight Notes

1. Are you willing to change your thoughts?

2. Can you help your child help you raise him/her?

3. What actions steps have you taken to help your child be positive?

*Please send any questions or topics for discussions to: tenwaystohelp@gmail.com

CHAPTER 9

It's A Mind Thing

AS A MAN thinketh so is he. This famous saying is used as a business foundation for many important books. We shape, frame, and believe who we are by what we have been told. But, what do we say to ourselves about who we are? The old paradigms of being too tall, too short, too large, too small, stay with us even as we develop into our adulthood. The good news is that it is not too late to change our perceptions about ourselves. You really can think about whom you are and what you want to become and become it, just because you are saying and believing it. It all begins with you controlling what you think.

TEACH YOUR CHILDREN TO SEE BEYOND THEMSELVES.
What you visualize and the images you create are what you think about and how you think about yourself. Each person needs to have the vision of them accomplishing their goals. That is why life coach trainers have clients make vision boards. If you can see it then you will believe it and it will become a reality. I have had people who have said everything they put on their vision board they accomplished. They even put a van on there they wanted for their family. This family actually put an ad on Craigslist asking if anyone had a van they wanted to give away for a family of eight who needed a good vehicle. Someone gave them a van. They just believed for it and got it. There is hope in believing. As human beings we are made to be hopeful. I have a little saying, "What you see is not my finish." If a person's mindset is towards achieving then that person will finish his/her goals.

A MINDSET TO OVERCOME OBSTACLES.
Obstacles will be your biggest adversary. You must be willing to confront your conflicts and keep your mind set forward. Your children are watching you. You are part of their inspiration. A large part of parenting is modeling doing the right thing. They see your struggles and they see how you handle them. Your children need to know that they can work through their obstacles because they see you work through your obstacles. Some of the obstacles are mistakes that we made. A modeling of forgiveness needs to be visibly in place. Your children need to know that we all will make mistakes. We make corrections. We forgive, let go, and continue to move forward with the mindset of being successful. Without these steps in place, you continue to rehearse the hurt and take a seat standing in the past.

OBSTACLES HELP US DEFINE AND DISCIPLINE OUR CHARACTER.
As parents we are still in the school of learning. We are still passing tests to move to the next grade. Each obstacle requires tenacity and builds a resilience to move forward. What we knew in the third grade is not enough

information to pass the test in the fourth grade. So, we are constantly gathering information about ourselves and how we integrate knowledge to overcome the obstacles of life. I often say, "You cannot get through life without going through life." As long as you are alive, life issues are not avoidable. You can choose to have a mindset to use obstacles to develop character. We must see ourselves beyond our present situation.

LIKE CHILDREN WE MUST DREAM AND HAVE VISIONS FOR OUR FUTURE TO MOVE FORWARD.

This energy moves us from the past and the present to our future goals. What is fascinating about children is their ability to dream and to imagine. They can take a toy and create a story having enormous amounts of enjoyment. That is the part of our personality that we need to keep alive as parents. We need to dream for ourselves, our children, and for our family. Your children are looking for the fun part in you. I heard a five-year-old request help for his parent's situation. Their childhood dreams carry the weights of their parents because they know the family business. As parents, we need to be adults and deal with our issues and allow our children to be children.

Referencing "Rich Dad Poor Dad": In the book, *Rich Dad, Poor Dad*, one father was a college professor who always said they did not have money for this and they did not have money for that. Money was a very bad subject. This dad was called the poor dad, his dad. The father who always said we will see how we can do that. Let's figure out a way to pay for that. He was called Rich dad, his friend's dad. These dads had two completely different mindsets. Rich dad was willing to learn. He was willing to explore different avenues to make something different happened. The poor dad, even though he was very well educated had a mindset of a logical reality. It is what it is. He was not willing to learn beyond what his logic manifested. His fear of the unknown was an inhibitor in playing the role of an obstacle for him and his family.

We cannot let fear be the driver of our dreams because fear will drive the dreams away. The rich dad knew he would find a way to be rich. That was part of his imagination. He was going to pursue until it became a reality. He worked on learning new ways to have his money make money for him. Be willing to change your mind. Change your ways and change the way you do things. You cannot continuously do the same things over and over again and expect different results. If you want something different to happen you must do something different. We so often tell our children they can do or be anything they what to be. What have we done in our modeling to validate that statement? Do they see us with gripping fears and stressed with life issues? Are we showing them yes, life has issues but this is how we deal with it. This is how we resolve our issues. Have a new mindset where you are willing to be creative and explorative will be required for success. Parents need to use their imaginations like they did when they played with toys. Just create all kinds of scenarios. Your children create and order how the outcome of the story will be. This is the same modeling we need to do as parents. Show them you can create your own story from the start to the finish. You can speak into your own life. Walk through the process of change and change as needed. Embrace change so that you can experience different results. It is only a change of mind!

Gardner's Theory of Multiple Intelligences (MI) (1943), profiles an individuals' cognitive developmental process. Even though Vygotsky (1896/1978), and Gardner (1943), were two different theorists who lived in different times and different parts of the country, they are very similar. Vygotsky's Zone of Proximal Development which states, the child can learn above where he is developmentally, connects with Gardner's MI. If you understand the child's intelligences, you can move him/her beyond where his/her developmental stage is currently. Piaget (1896/1980) believed in stages of development. The child learns according to his age. Gardner in *Frames of Mind: The Theory of Multiple Intelligences (1943)*, being a protégé of Piaget, believed in the stages and congruently all three theorists agreed on developmental stages, but Gardner (1943) moves beyond the uniformity of group stage movement. Children can maximize above their developmental stage and the specificity of a child's forte is given special nurturing at that time. The goal is to move children beyond what is expected and cheer them on to use their mind.

Chapter Nine Notes

1. How can you help your child think beyond what they see?

   _____
   _____
   _____
   _____
   _____
   _____

2. Are you modeling how to work through obstacles?

   _____
   _____
   _____
   _____
   _____
   _____

3. What steps are you taking to encourage your child's dreams?

   _____
   _____
   _____
   _____
   _____
   _____

*Please send any questions or topics for discussions to: tenwaystohelp@gmail.com

CHAPTER 10

Can't Go – Can't Grow....Can't Grow – Can't Go

When you release fear you can hear. There is a certain amount of clarity where the mind processes when there is no fear. You can practice clearing your mind. Find out what detoxes you. What de-escalates you? For some people it is just sitting still and breathing. For others, playing music de-escalates them. Some people relate by reading. Other people take a drive or walk. It is essential as a parent that you continue to cleanse your mind. Your mind has to be like a garden that is able to grow. We are thinking being. Our processing comes from our thoughts. We need to consciously control our thinking. This means learning how to engage positive thoughts and edit negative thoughts. It is a choice what thoughts you think. Choose nurturing thoughts to help you grow.

We even think when we are asleep. I was working with one of my clients and asking what she does before she goes to bed. She replied that she thinks about everything that she has to do the next day. Sometimes she evaluates if her day was successful and how upsetting that was. As a result, she cannot slow down her mind and does not sleep well in general. Because our minds are in continuous motion it is important how we set our minds before we rest. If you are watching intense television shows or thinking about intense situations, it will affect your rest. Positive influences are needed before you go to bed so that you can rest. Most of us have been exposed to knowing it is a good thing to read pleasant stories to our children before they go to bed. But, unfortunately, some children have never been read to. Reading to your children helps you to connect their imagination.

Before my five children left for college, there were two books I read to them out loud. Keep in mind; these were 18-year-old children. There were two books I wanted them to hear in my voice, so my voice would be in their heads. Because the mind is so magnificent, everything you say to your children is recorded in their minds. At some point it will come to the forefront. That is why it is so important to watch the words that you say. The two books of my choice were Kiyosaki's, *Rich Dad Poor Dad*

Ten Ways to Help Your Child Overcome Obstacles

and Ben Carson's, *Gentle Hands*. They both are stories about how you can grow and go. If you do not go, you will never grow. These were stories of persons using their imaginative creation and becoming successful beyond all logic. I wanted to open my children's world of imagination to growing.

In order to grow you have to be willing to take what looks like a risk. But, actually is a greater risk if you do not do it because you will never grow. Now, all five of my children are interacting in business on a global scale. I wanted them to be boundless in their thinking and exposure in their promise and purpose. They needed to believe and know that they were purposeful human beings. This is the reason why they were so unique with only one identifiable voiceprint and fingerprint. They were created for a specific reason and a specific purpose. They would need to be willing to grow and go to arrive at their purpose.

You never stop growing and if you do, you will never arrive at your purpose. Life unfolds into many turns un-expectantly. But, it is all purposeful. If you can release your fear and visualize in your mind and your heart how this is working out for your good, you can stay positive and

say affirmative things daily to help yourself. You will reach those goals. Training your child to have a strong constitution and becoming strong in their commitment will carry them when they have to move and go as one.

Some parts of the journey we will travel alone. We need to be strong enough to make it. Read stories in sheer conversations with your child about heroes from your life and how you were encouraged to move forward. If you do not have any, get some books and create some so that you have something to share about whom you respect. Looking at the life of George Washington Carver who overcame surmountable obstacles is just remarkable considering the time in history. He did not allow his past to stymie or predict his future. He knew, if he was going to grow in his purpose he would go far beyond his present possibilities.

> It is rare to find a man of the caliber of George Washington Carver. A man who would decline an invitation to work for a salary of more than $100,000 a year (almost a million today) to continue his research on behalf of his countrymen.
>
> As an agricultural chemist, Carver discovered 300 uses for peanuts and hundreds more uses for soybeans, pecans, and sweet potatoes. Among the listed items that he suggested to southern farmers to help them economically were his recipes and improvements to/for: adhesives, axle grease, bleach, buttermilk, chili sauce, fuel briquettes, ink, instant coffee, linoleum, mayonnaise, meat tenderizer, metal polish, paper, plastic, pavement, shaving cream, shoe polish, synthetic rubber, talcum powder and wood stain. Once, he testified before the Senate Agriculture Committee, saying that he got his knowledge of peanuts from the Bible. When asked what the Bible said about peanuts he replied, "The Bible does not teach anything regarding the peanut. But, it told me about God and God told me about the peanut."

Personal Present Perspective. If you cannot see it, you will not believe it and you will not be it. It is about visualization, conceptualization, and realization. At an early age your children must be able to see where they can grow and go. They need to have a perspective about their future that is hopeful. You need to be that support system that gives them sustainability to know they can do this. Share love and respect with your children so that they can be healed from their fears. Share questions and unanswered questions with your children. They need to know that you can be that friend who does not have all the answers. You are going to process the answers with them together.

Sail boat: In order for the sail boat to sail the winds have to blow. No one will go through life without winds blowing in their life. Just know that the winds are moving you forward toward your destiny. The only thing that will sink the boat is the water within the boat. Be careful whom you embrace into your inner circle and in your inner dream. Train your children in their early stages of life to use wisdom in choosing their friends. Every one cannot sit in your boat. As I was training my children in this, I was training myself. It has taken me a lifetime to learn that everyone is not there to help your boat float.

Every Apple seed can create an apple tree. Every acorn can become a great oak tree. Your seed is there inside you. Make it your choice how to nurture it and grow it. You get to decide your level of success. You are responsible for the time you spend on this planet. Teach your children that success is a choice. If you do not succeed, it is because you have given away your power. Take back your power making decisions about yourself. It depends completely on you.

Challenges form obstacles creating possibilities. With faith, hope, and belief, one can overcome obstacles to grow and go beyond impossibilities. Help your children to visualize far beyond what they see and become that entity of one that creates boundless greatness! Parents… You can do this!

Chapter Ten Notes

1. Are you growing as a family?

2. Do you expose you child to different career choices?

3. What actions are you taking to encourage your child to live fearlessly?

*Please send any questions or topics for discussions to: tenwaystohelp@gmail.com

References

Bandura, A. (1989). Human agency in social cognitive theory. *American Psychologist, 44,* 1175– 1184. http://dx.doi.org/10.1037//0003-066X.44.9.1175 Bitter, J. R., Long, L. L., & Young, M. E. (2010). *Introduction to marriage, couple, and family counseling.* (Laureate Education, Inc., custom ed.). Mason, OH: Cengage Learning

Bruner, J. J. (1996). *The culture of education.* Cambridge, MA: Harvard University Press.

Federer, W. J. (2008). *George Washington Carver-His Life and Faith in His Own Words.* Library of Congress.

Dean, R. (1995). A narrative approach to groups. *Clinical Social Work Journal,* 23, 287-304.

Erikson, E. H. (1950). *Childhood and society.* New York, NY: W.W. Norton & Company, Inc.

Gardner, H. (1983). *Frames of mind: The theory of multiple intelligences.* New York: Basic Books.

Garrin. J. (2013). From college student to change agent: A triadic model of self-efficacy, attribution, and appraisal. *Journal of Social Change, 5,* 40–57. http://dx.doi.org/10.5590/ JOSC.2013.05.1.04

Gore, J. S., & Wilburn, K. (2010). A regional culture model of academic achievement: Comparing Appalachian and non-Appalachian students in Kentucky. *Journal Of Social, Evolutionary, and Cultural Psychology, 4,* 156–173. http://dx.doi.org/10.1037/h0099292

Helmstetter, S. (1982). *What To Say When You Talk to Yourself.* Pocket Books. New York, N.Y.

Keene, S. (2008). Listening to students: Higher education and the American Dream: Why the "status quo" won't get us there. *Change, 40*(6), 65–66. Retrieved from http:// www.changemag.org/index.html

Keller, H. (2011). Culture and cognition: Developmental perspectives. *Journal of Cognitive Education and Psychology, 10*(1) 3–8. http://dx.doi.org/10.1891/1945- 8959.10.1.3

Kiyosaki, R. (2012). *Rich Dad Poor Dad.* Plata Publishing, LLC Scottsdale Arizona 85251

Piaget, J. (1896/1980). Piaget's theory of cognitive development. Barry J. Wadsworth. New York, NY: Longman.

White, M. (1986). Negative explanation, restraint, and double description: A template for family therapy. *Family Process, 25, 169-184.*

Ventegodt, S., Merrick, and Anderson, N.N. (2003). Quality of life theory III. Maslow revsited. *The Scientific World Journa*l 3,1050-1057

Vygotsky, L. (1978). *Mind in society.* Cambridge, MA: Harvard University Press.

Autism: A Parent, A Teacher, A Professor's Perspective

5 THINGS YOU SHOULD NOT DO- Parent: Kelly Nissley

Never shelter your child.
Kids on the spectrum have a hard time socializing but that does not mean to keep them in a bubble. There are many actives you can take them to which also incorporates socializing. Here are a few ideas listed that children enjoy whether on the spectrum or not.

    The zoo
    Indoor waterpark
    Chuck E cheese
    A park

My experience as a mother with a child on the spectrum with socializing can be quite difficult at times. My son never wanted to leave the house. Going to the grocery store could be a challenge. What I learned is he did a lot better if we went first thing in the morning before it got to busy. Taking your child to the zoo can be a challenge also. I would take a stroller it made him feel more comfortable. I would turn it into a game for him. What would you like to see and we would proceed to find whichever animal he wanted to see on the map and head out. Eventually he would come out of the stroller excited to see the animals and would hop back in the stroller to head to the next one with eventually not even using the stroller. With every situation on socializing try to be creative and come up with a fun, plan.

Never let anyone else be your voice
As a parent you know your child better than anyone else. When it comes to childcare and schools you need to be the voice for your child. You must be very strong and assertive as to what you expect for your child. When it comes to schools and IEP'S as a parent you can tell the school what you expect don't just sit back and allow the schools to make all the decisions for you. If you don't agree with anything you must say something and

make the change. Only you know what's right for your child and where you want to see your child succeed in.

When It's time for the yearly IEP update on my son, I carefully read what the school has wrote down what their plans and goals are for my son. If I feel there is more areas of focus I want them to work on I make it very clear (example reading) that I want his reading level to be increased by our next meeting. I will not sign the IEP papers till my areas of focus are addressed and included on the IEP'S goals.

Never speak for your child
Children on the spectrum have a difficult time with language and can get easily frustrated. There are many things available to make this a lot easier with less frustration.

Teach your child sign language. As your child learns the sign language say the word when your child does the sign.

Make pictures and place on the cabinets. When your child wants something and points to the picture say the word

Electronic Talking Device. Parents can make pictures and program the device and every time you child press on of the buttons it will say what it is.

Make a Picture Book. You can use a little photo album to place pictures inside it. The internet has thousands of images you can print from food to toys. Print out the photos and use Velcro to place in your book. Your child then is able to look through the book and pull out the picture of the item and hand to you

As a mother with two sons on the spectrum, language was the hardest. As I would watch my sons get more frustrated while trying to communicate with me and I just couldn't understand what they were trying to say. I thought to myself why couldn't I teach them sign language and I would know exactly what they wanted, so that's what I did. I would pick a very simple sign (blanket which was to hands together on the side of the face. Once my son did the sign for blanket I always said the word blanket with the sign) and began teaching it. It took no time at all for them to pick up on the signs and even starting making their own for toys etc and the frustration almost disappeared and that's when I put pictures of all their favorite food on the cabinets where the food was located. When my son decided he would want crackers, he would go the the cabinet and point and I could then point to the crackers and say do you want crackers. I would repeat these words over and over and they stated to repeat me with the words and before long sign language and pictures was replaced with actual words.

Never use your child being on the spectrum be an excuse for their bad behavior
Children on the spectrum will have their special moments (meltdowns) due to change in routines, frustration and or they are just having a bad day. The key here is to recognize the difference between a meltdown or just bad behavior. Children on the spectrum do display regular bad behaviors, not listening, talking back, using wrong choice of words and need to be corrected for this behavior and not using being on the spectrum as the reason. These children are very smart and also know the difference between right and wrong.

My two children on the spectrum would display regular bad behaviors and you have to really focus on the difference between the "TRUE" meltdown or bad behavior. The best example I can give on this one was we were at a birthday party, my son wanted some cake and it wasn't time yet, so he threw himself to the floor kicking and screaming, well this is just regular bad behavior. It was due to the situation of too many people overwhelming him he became uncomfortable. He was not thinking about cake but seeing it started his behavior. As soon as I said no to cake he started his bad behavior. These are the situations that you must think of what caused the reaction to know the true differences.

Never make your child feel any different than anyone else.
Children on the spectrum already have a sense that they are different and often struggle on why. As the parent you need to find ways to help eliminate this as much as possible. Find the areas your child succeeds in and drive them further with it. Encourage after school activities and sports. If the child is a toddler set up playdates with other children, siblings, cousins, etc. with an activity your child has picked out.

My son eventually got to where he was asking if he was different or stupid. This was very hard to hear. When I had asked why is he asking if he is stupid he would come back and say cause he couldn't do what other kids were doing with schoolwork. All I could do as a mother was sit down with him and have a nice talk about how he is not different. All kids learn at a different rate. I also tried explaining that there are some kids that are on a higher learning level and some that are even on a lower learning level than what he was on but all children are still the same and no one is different because of that. I would continue weekly talks with him asking how he was feeling and how he thought he was doing in school. I could start to see the confidence he was developing in himself and no longer thinking he was different.

Intervention Specialist: The Teacher–Natasha Abbas

1. A parent needs to expect their child to succeed. No matter what set their standards high with or without Autism they can strive for excellence.

One statement that was made by someone who leads a group focusing on their children who have Autism, stated, "She would be happy if her child just got a job with bagging groceries." That is exactly how she worded it. This person is powerful and respected by a lot of people and if she says that, then everyone who listens to her will set the same exact mindset and standards for their child who has Autism. I feel that is not the way a parent should look at Autism. When parents set their child's expectations high, with or without Autism, the parent need to help their child believe in themselves. As a parent, children need to be accountable for their own success. Do not allow Autism to be an excuse for low success standards. With higher expectancy your child will strive. The outcome will be positive and your child will have a higher success rate. Keep in mind that when things get hard help your child strive towards excellence. Never give up or lose hope in your child! I always tell my students how smart they are and that no matter what they can always accomplish their goals and dreams.

2. Parent(s) need to challenge their child who has Autism.

No matter what challenge your child who has Autism. If they kick, hit, spit, say mean words still show compassion, do not get offended with what they say and hold your ground. Parents need to remain strong, do not cave in and let them get away with things that they should not get away with; if you believe what they are doing is not ok follow your heart. Even if it is harsh love, do it because in the end this will help your child. I have a nonverbal student. During the first couple of times he came, he would cry as his grandma left the school building. When he was in public schools the school would call his grandparents every single day because he would have a fit at school and they did not want to deal with him. He would get so nervous that he would throw up and the school would send him home. The reason why he would throw up was because he knew that was his ticket home. Now that he comes to CASS MIND Academy he has been coming two times a week and stays the whole school day and he loves it! What CASS MIND Academy did was do home visits at the student's and grandparents place. As time went on there was success.

3. Parents need to make sure that their child with Autism experiences new and different experiences and people. Do not take away their experiences. Try not to convince schools to take your child out of challenges.

This statement means that your child needs to go out into the world and experience as many things as possible. The more your child is left in the house and does not interact with anyone; your child will have a hard time in the future. For example: going to a job shadow and interacting with other people. Other healthy experiences: going to the grocery store with an adult and ask someone to help find something in the store, ordering their own food at a restaurant. Also, interacting in group activities. In the past I have heard people talking about how their child stresses out in gym because the whistle is to loud. A parent said, "Oh you can have in their IEP that they do not like gym because of loud noises and get your child out of gym." The parent responded, "but I do not want my child to be taken out of something, that could help her." I completely agree with what she said. Your child needs to stay in what they are struggling with, just getting them out of what they are uncomfortable with does not help them. It allows them to have an excuse and it shows that it is ok to run away from what they are afraid of. No parent should allow those thoughts to be in their child's head. So, challenge yourself to allow your child who has Autism to challenge themselves into new experiences, even if you have to force them to do it. My youngest student who was five years old at the time, held onto his mom's leg tight, kicked, hit, bit, when his mom would leave. He would hide underneath the table and not come out for forty minutes. For the next couple of days he would do the same exact thing every morning. But as time went on he got better and better. His mom could have quit right there and said since he is doing poorly I will not let him go back to school and have him homeschooled. However, she made him go to school and as time went on he became more comfortable and was more happy. Also, as his teacher I was patient, I allowed him to have his fits because as time went on, he got to know me better and was more comfortable. Also, as time went on his "melt downs" were shorter and then they ended up not happening at all. Now in the present he has not had any melt downs in the last couple months. He talks constantly, makes jokes, laughs and even though he is the youngest he is a firecracker and quite a leader!

4. Your child needs to reach out of their comfort zones, interact with social clubs, college experiences, and interactions with anything that is not part of their norm.

In today's society people view Autism as a weakness, I view Autism as a strength, an opportunity to show the world that they are able to come out of their comfort zones, develop their own thoughts and be successful. Allowing your child to go to different social clubs and scheduling college visits at a young age, shapes their mindset, at a young age that they can go somewhere in life. The younger one starts, setting high standards the better mindset your child can have, to be able to focus on working hard, to interact with others, to be successful and experience what "normal people" experience. At CASS MIND Academy when a new person comes into the school, they shake their hand, look them in the eyes and introduces themselves to the visitor. By doing this they are out of their comfort zones.

5. Parents need to be patient and give them time for growth in independence, create their own actions, allow them to make their own experiences and learn from them.

As a parent, with any child you always want to protect them, you do not want them to be hurt or feel struggle. But when you let your child be independent they learn how to problem solve and think critically for themselves. They learn how to take action and fix their own problems. As a parent, mom and/or dad takes notice when their child makes the same exact mistakes all the time, remain patient for example have a discussion every week with your child. Ask them questions, how did you handle certain situations? Did you solve a certain situation the best way you could? How can you better improve these struggles? By having a discussion every week, you help your child; because they can develop their own self talk and self awareness as time goes on and they make this a habit. The more you ask them these questions the more they will notice. They will start asking themselves these questions and they start taking notice about what they did right and ways they need to improve. This allows them to have their own experiences, which allows them to be more independent.

6. Do not allow your child who has Autism or any type of disability not accomplish something they are good at because they are different from society's view of what a true successful person looks like, acts like or does.

As a teacher I always challenge them to work harder, to be a better version of themselves, to feel important. I challenge every single one of my students to feel, to feel accomplished, to feel successful and to feel happy. As their teacher I make sure I express every single emotion so they develop a form of empathy and I educate them on watching what they say because it can hurt someone. I am also a sensitive person and through the years I have taught myself how to control my emotions by writing, by working out and by talking with a close friends or my husband. I strongly suggest to all my students to talk to someone they are close to, so they express their feelings and emotions and I show that it is ok to be a sensitive person but to not allow others to take advantage of your sensitivity.

As a child my parents always encouraged me to work hard and do my best. When I was a toddler I did not talk and the school was testing me to see "what was wrong with me." At one point the testing people thought I had Mental Retardation, which they called it back in the 90's, now it is called Intellectual Disability, second time around they thought I had Autism and third time around they determined it was a Learning Disability. The only factor that they considered was because I would not talk. I understand how it feels to struggle, to feel like you are not smart, to feel like you cannot make it. But as a parent you can help your child see what they can not see, to encourage them, to say they are smart and be their support, most importantly to let your child know that they can make it and succeed. No matter what people say, do not let that define you as you, you define yourself and if you believe in your child and help them believe in themselves then anything is possible.

7. Never lose hope. Love them no matter what.

When someone enters into CASS MIND Academy, we always provide a sense of hope and love for the children and their parents. There are many parents who come tired and unhappy with their child and with how the school systems have been handling different situations with their child. I have heard many stories about children being bullied by other students and sometimes by teachers, how they are failing every subject and how they have been constantly misbehaving because they are struggling. When their child comes into a different learning environment, such as CASS MIND Academy they do better because it is more individualized and we are able to reach every single students needs. As time goes on their child works harder. As the teacher I treat every student as a mature student, with high expectations, who expects them to make it, who expects them to work hard. I am not ok with mediocre, I expect my students to work hard, gain dedication and learn to have passion. This is what helps people reach their dreams and even when one reaches their dreams, they have to keep going and that is what CASS MIND Academy expects from their students. No matter what parents should never lose hope and know that there are people out there who will support and help lift them up when they are down about their child. When parents are at their lowest points the people who love them most will help. So therefore never lose hope and love always.

A story I would like to share about my student, One of my student's had such a harsh childhood, he was physically and emotionally abused. The students were bullying him and the adults did not stick up for him. The adults were not understanding for him and as his parents kept fighting for a better education for him, the school was calling home telling him that he was misbehaving and being bad. That he needed to be picked up for being rude and being bad. The school he attended were just giving up on him treating him like he was a lost cause. But to me he was not he was a student who needed a safe haven, a student who needed to feel loved and wanted, a student who wanted to feel respected by adults, a person of importance and value. All of those things are normal things to want, to feel accepted! As he started coming to CASS MIND Academy, as his teacher I wanted to get to know him as a student, see what ways worked best for his learning skills, in what ways did he socialize, what annoyed him and how he reacted to situations he liked being in and situations he did not like as much. As I got to know this student I noticed how he was helpful, loving and he cares so much about others, sometimes more than himself. He has a humongous heart! This student means well and even though he makes mistakes. This student has a loving personality, cares about his classmates and all the adults at his school. This student has been working hard improving in all subjects and his social skills. At CASS MIND Academy is now his safe haven, a place he can feel relaxed, be honest, be happy, smile and a place where his hope was gained. So no one should want to take that away from him, right!?

8. Show ways that you as their parent are proud of them.

It could be anything from saying good job for working hard in school, to tying their own shoes, to being able to socialize with others. Also, becoming better communicators, to working hard and being happy. At CASS MIND Academy the parents always comment about how well their child is doing and how they are happy with their child's behavior. But some parents may struggle with being proud of their child especially if they struggle with accepting that their child has Autism. There was a family who visited CASS MIND Academy and the parents stated, "we do not use that word," the word that they were referring to was Autism. They do not like stating their child has Autism. I completely understand being protective parents but do not hide them from the truth, This family struggled with facing the struggles of their child, having a label and being more concerned about what society thought about their child instead of just focusing on what they thought about their child. Autism is part of who they are, never be ashamed, instead be proud. Say, "yes my child has Autism, but that's ok, we will get through everything and do it together. It could be anything from saying good job for working hard in school, to tying their own shoes, to being able to socialize with others.

These are pointers that are important to share and are important to keep in mind when one is feeling down. Always expect your child to succeed, challenge your child and expose your child to as many life experiences as possible. Also, make sure your child interacts with others and reaches out of their comfort zones. Allow your child to experience success. Never lose hope, always love and show how proud you are to be their parent and have them as your child!`

Stress and Health in Parents of Individuals with Autism Spectrum Disorders
Jen D. Wong, Ph.D.

The purpose of this section is to provide an overview of the literature on stress and health in parents of individuals with autism spectrum disorders.

Stress and Health

In contrast to other types of family caregiving (e.g., caregiving for a parent or spouse with a health condition), providing care for a child with an autism spectrum disorder (ASD) often is a lifelong process that persists into midlife and late adulthood. While prior research has showed evidence of resiliency in the caregiving process (e.g., Bekhet, Johnson, & Zauszniewski, 2012), the unique nature of parenting a child with ASD often translates into greater psychological and physical challenges when compared to parents of children without disabilities (Cadman et al., 2012; Hayes & Watson, 2013 for a review). Not only are parents of individuals with ASD more likely to report greater exposure to daily stressors (e.g., child behavior problems) than parents of children without disabilities, these parents also are reporting more days with headaches, backaches, and fatigue (Smith et al., 2010; Smith, Seltzer, & Greenberg, 2012). Furthermore, the rate of depression has been documented to be higher in mothers of children with ASD than in mothers of typically developing children (Sawyer et al., 2010).

In addition to these psychological and physical challenges, parents of individuals with ASD are more likely to experience dysregulation in physiological functioning. In the recent years, there has been an increasing number of studies investigating family-related factors and cortisol reactivity (e.g., Dykens & Lambert, 2013; Seltzer et al., 2010). Cortisol is the main product of the hypothalamic–pituitary–adrenal (HPA) axis (Adam & Gunnar, 2001) and is considered to be a general indicator of neuroendocrine regulation. Under conditions of threat or distress, the HPA axis activates and secretes cortisol (Dickerson & Kemeny, 2004).

When activated, cortisol helps the body adapt to the environment and maintain homeostasis through various processes including the stabilization of glucose levels, cell metabolism, and inflammatory responses (Heim, Ehlert, & Hellhammer, 2000). The cortisol awakening response is a distinct part of the diurnal pattern of cortisol and is considered a reliable marker of the HPA axis (Clow, Thorn, Evans, & Hucklebridge, 2004; Hellhammer et al., 2007). The decline in cortisol at the end of the day has been equated to the body's way of regulating its system throughout the day and restoring its system in preparation for the challenges of the next day (Ice et al., 2004).

The chronic stress of parenting a child with a developmental disability has been shown to result in an atypical pattern of cortisol in the context of challenging care-related events. In their study, Seltzer and colleagues (2009) found that parents of adolescents and adults with disabilities exhibited a flatter daily decline of cortisol on days when they spent more time with their child with a disability, a pattern that was not observed in parents of children without disabilities. Similarly, a profile of blunted or flattened cortisol was evident in a sample of mothers of individuals with ASD (Seltzer et al., 2010) such that if the individual with an ASD had a history of clinically significant behavior problems, the mother exhibited a less pronounced cortisol awakening response on the morning after a day when the individual with ASD had more behavior problems. The observed diminished adrenal activity is in line with reports of blunted or flattened cortisol responses in individuals with chronic disease conditions, certain forms of depression, and post-traumatic stress disorder (Pruessner, Hellhammer, & Kirschbaum, 1999; Yehuda, 2000). Although these studies illustrated a pattern of flattened or blunted cortisol profile in parents of individuals with disabilities, the work of Wong, Mailick, Greenberg, Hong, & Coe (2014) showed that the source of the stressors may differentially impact cortisol reactivity. Wong and colleagues (2014) found that while mothers of adolescents and adults with developmental disabilities (e.g., ASD, Fragile X syndrome) had *lower* overall awakening cortisol level than the comparison group, these mothers also had *elevated* levels of awakening cortisol on mornings following a stressful work day. Thus, the study highlights the need for further examination of the ways in which different sources of stressors may impact the health of parents experiencing chronic caregiving demands.

Support and Health
Social support holds an important role in buffering the relationship between stress and health in the study of parents of children with ASD. Prior studies generally have showed higher levels of social support to be related to lower levels of depressive symptoms and negative mood as well as higher levels of positive mood (Bishop, Richler, Cain, & Lord, 2007; Ekas, Lickenbrock, & Whitman, 2010; Pottie, Cohen, & Ingram, 2009). It is important to note that social support is not all the same. In their sample of mothers of adolescents and adults with ASD, Smith, Greenberg, & Seltzer (2012) found that higher levels of *negative* support (e.g., criticized the mother's involvement in her child's life, made excessive demands on the mother) from members in their social network were linked to greater negative affect and depressive symptoms. In another study of parents of children with ASD, Gouin, da Estrela, Desmarais, & Barker (2016) found that the *source* of social support received was predictive of C-reactive protein (CRP), which is a biomarker of inflammation. Specifically, greater levels of informal social support (e.g., friends, family) and formal support services (e.g., respite care, physical therapy) were related to lower levels of CRP. Considering that elevated levels of CRP have been linked to poorer health (e.g., Christian et al., 2011), having multiple sources of social support may help combat stress-induced immune system dysregulation. Thus, these findings highlight the important need to consider the quality and source of social support when navigating caregiving stress.

Take Home Message
Based on these findings, we have identify ways in which parents can help to protect and enhance their health and well-being.

1. Recognize Stress: In order to improve one's health, it is important to first recognize that one is experiencing stress. This recommendation seems simple but individuals often do not realize that they are under stress. Given the amount of daily responsibilities associated with caring for a son/daughter with ASD, parents are constantly 'on the go' whether it is dealing with a change in routine or navigating schedules. Being 'on the go' may not allow parents the opportunity to recognize that they are stressed; thus, taking a moment to acknowledge stress is an important first step to improving caregivers' health.
2. Identify Source of Stress: Consider that a person's life is comprised of different domains (e.g., family, work), identifying the source(s) of stressors is key to manage stressors more effectively. Importantly, these different life domains may intersect with each other (e.g., work to family spillover); thus, determining the areas of life that are resulting in greater stressors will ultimately help caregivers better navigate their stress.
3. Seek Quality Support: It can be very challenging for a caregiver to find support when navigating every day caregiving responsibilities. However, it is important to keep in mind that not all social support is the same, and that both the quality and source of social support matter. Technology (e.g., social networking sites/groups) may offer parents a tool to promote social support. Through social networking sites, parents can maintain their connection to their family and friends, as well as seek out support from other parents of children with ASD in their community in the efforts to help promote their quality of life.

References

Adam, E. K. & Gunnar, M. R. (2001). Relationship functioning and home and work demands predict individual differences in diurnal cortisol patterns in women. *Psychoneuroendocrinology, 26,* 189-208.

Bekhet, A. K., Johnson, N. L., & Zauszniewski, J. A. (2012). Resilience in family members of persons with autism spectrum disorder: A review of the literature. *Issues in Mental Health Nursing, 33,* 650-656.

Bishop, S. L., Richler, J., Cain, A. C., & Lord, C. (2007). Predictors of perceived negative impact in mothers of children with autism spectrum disorder. *American Journal on Mental Retardation, 112,* 450-461.

Cadman, T., Eklund, H., Howley, D., Hayward, H., Clarke, H., Findon, J., ... Glaser, K. (2012). Caregiver burden as people with autism spectrum disorder and attention-deficit/hyperactivity disorder transition into adolescence and adulthood in the United Kingdom. Journal of the American Academy of Child & Adolescent Psychiatry, *51,* 879-888.

Christian, L. M., Glaser, R., Porter, K., Malarkey, W. B., Beversdorf, D., & Kiecolt-Glaser, J. K. (2011). Poorer self-rated health is associated with elevated inflammatory markers among older adults. *Psychoneuroendocrinology, 36,* 1495-1504.

Clow, A., Thorn, L., Evans P., & Hucklebridge, F. (2004). The awakening cortisol response: methodological issues and significance. *Stress, 7,* 29-37.

Dickerson, S. S., & Kemeny, M. E. (2004). Acute stressors and cortisol responses: A theoretical integration and synthesis of laboratory research. *Psychological Bulletin, 130,* 355-391.

Dykens, E. M., & Lambert, W. (2013). Trajectories of diurnal cortisol in mothers of children with autism and other developmental disabilities: Relations to health and mental health. *Journal of Autism and Developmental Disorders, 43,* 2426-2434.

Ekas, N. V., Lickenbrock, D. M., & Whitman, T. L. (2010). Optimism, social support, and well-being in mothers of children with autism spectrum disorder. *Journal of Autism and Developmental Disorders, 40,* 1274–1284.

Gouin, J. P., da Estrela, C., Desmarais, K., & Barker, E. T. (2016). **The impact of formal and informal support on health in the context of caregiving stress.** *Family Relations, 65,* 191-206.

Hayes, S. A., & Watson, S. L. (2013). The impact of parenting stress: A meta-analysis of studies comparing the experience of parenting stress in parents of children with and without autism spectrum disorder. Journal of Autism and Developmental Disorders, *43,* 629–642.

Heim, C., Ehlert, U., & Hellhammer, D. H. (2000). The potential role of hypocortisolism in the pathophysiology of stress-related bodily disorders, *Psychoneuroendocrinology, 25,* 1-35.

Hellhammer, J., Fries, E., Schweisthal, O. W., Schlotz, W., Stone, A. A., & Hagemann, D. (2007). Several daily measurements are necessary to reliably assess the cortisol rise after awakening: State- and trait components. *Psychoneuroendocrinology, 32,* 80-86.

Ice, G. H., Katz-Stein, A., Himes, J., & Kane, R. L. (2004). Diurnal cycles of salivary cortisol in older adults. *Psychoneuroendocrinology, 29,* 355-370.

Pottie, C. G., Cohen, J., & Ingram, K. M. (2009). Parenting a child with autism: Contextual factors associated with enhanced daily parental mood. *Journal of Pediatric Psychology, 34*, 419-429.

Pruessner, J. C, Hellhammer, D. H., & Kirschbaum, C. (1999). Burnout, perceived stress, and cortisol response to awakening. *Psychosomatic Medicine, 61*, 197-204.

Sawyer, M. J., Bittman, M. L. A., Greca, A. M., Crettenden, A. D., Harchak, T. F., & Martin, J. (2010). Time demands of caring for children with autism: What are the implications for maternal mental health? *Journal of Autism and Developmental Disorders, 40*, 620-628.

Seltzer, M. M., Almeida, D. M., Greenberg, J. S., Savla, J., Hong, J., & Taylor, J. L. (2009). Psychosocial and biological makers of daily lives of midlife parents of children with disabilities. *Journal of Health and Social Behavior, 50*, 1-15.

Seltzer, M. M., Greenberg, J. S., Hong, J., Smith, L., Almeida, D., Coe, C., & Stawski, R. S. (2010). Maternal cortisol levels and behavior problems in adolescents and adults with ASD. *Journal of Autism and Developmental Disorders, 40*, 457-69.

Smith, L., Hong, J., Seltzer, M. M., Greenberg, J. S., Almeida, D. M., & Bishop, S. (2010). Daily experiences among mothers of adolescents and adults with ASD. *Journal of Autism and Developmental Disorders, 40*, 167-78.

Smith, L. E., Seltzer, M. M., & Greenberg, J. S. (2012). Daily health symptoms of mothers of adolescents and adults with fragile X syndrome and mothers of adolescents and adults with autism spectrum disorder. *Journal of Autism and Developmental Disorders, 42*, 1836-46.

Smith, L. E., Greenberg, J. S., & Seltzer, M. M. (2012). Social support and well-being at mid-life among mothers of adolescents and adults with autism spectrum disorders. *Journal of Autism and Developmental Disorders, 42*, 1818-1826.

Wong, J. D., Mailick, M. R., Greenberg, J. S., Hong, J., & Coe, C. L. (2014). Daily work stress and awakening cortisol in mothers of adolescents and adults with autism spectrum disorders or fragile X syndrome. *Family Relations, 63* (1), 135-147.

Yehuda, R., Teicher, M. H., Trestman, R. L., Levengood, R. A., & Siever, L. J. (1996). Cortisol regulation in posttraumatic stress disorder and major depression: A chronobiological analysis. *Biological Psychiatry, 40*, 79-88.

Notes

Notes